Bird Sisters

For Natty with love.

*In memory of my mum Dawn Carol
who encouraged me to keep writing.*

Contents

Sisters (part i)   11
Bee Mornings   13
Feather Factory   14
Family Values   15
Snow   20
Winter at Daniel's Hole   21
The Piano Lesson   22
Sisters (part ii)   23
A Bird Inside   25
Quiet Man Norfolk   26
Night Feed   27
Sun Sister   28
Night Sickness   29
Our Father as a Horse   30
The Trap   31
Definitions (i)   32
From the Same Cloth   33
Counterpoint   34
Lent   35
Garden   36
After identifying your body   37
Water   38
Yare Song   40
Rain   41
The Drunkenness of Noah   43
Definitions (ii)   44
Thetford Forest   45
Something About the Light   46
The Callers   47

Gin Fox   49
Moldewarpe   50
Sparrow Sister   51
Oak   52
My owl sister mistakes me for a mouse   53
My owl sister pays me a visit   54
Clearing Out Mum   55
After cleaning out your house   56
Visiting Time   57
Operation   58
Maternity Ward   59
The Miracle   60
Breakdown   61
I have forgotten my password to you   63
no one speaks of you   64
This is how to fall   65
Bee Dress   66
Tickets to the Circus   67

Acknowledgements   71

"I am not averse to torching a place that is not habitable (so long as no one is inside). I will uncover a use for the ashes."

– C.D. Wright

Sisters (part i)

i.

This sister is the bones of the outfit,
she is the stuff that keeps the body up,
she is *dem bones, dem bones,*
she is calcified connective tissue,
she is femur, tibia, ulna, ribs.

ii.

This sister is the perfect scrunch
of English Rose,
all delicate petal curl, subtle pinks,
she opens her smile up to the sun.
This sister is a fuzzy stamen
with a dust of pollen,
she is the heady waft of perfume
begging you to bring your face down to her,
to bring your face right down.

iii.

She is the one with the hair just-so,
the handkerchief skirt hems, the well-cut clothes,
and on birthdays she gets the family all together –
we line up for photos that never looked posed,
and how she laughs at being vegetarian
but each Christmas allowing herself a little meat.

She is the one with the dainty features, the cutesy nose
the one they look for when you enter the room,
and the way they hang on her words makes you nauseous
but you can't say it, because she was the one
who watched out for you behind the shops and in the playground.

She is the one with the amicable divorce
and the books on cake decorating –
all those fiddly womanly things you have no patience for,
and she is the one who sat up all night in the crematorium
plaiting flowers into your mother's hair.

iv.

This sister reads Nietzsche,
her hair is twisted into bunches like tiny horns,
she makes abstract art with fur and feathers,
she likes to collect things from gutters and pavements,
and her eyes have that sparkle you were scared of as a kid.

v.

This sister is the bee
and we are the nectar,

she is drawing us in
with her persistent buzzing,

her talk of the hive mind,
her tremble dance.

Bee Mornings

The bees that sleep inside me
fill my mind with buzz.
We are Nectar they say,
we are Wax and Cone,
we are of Bee but not of Bee.

In the morning I look at my stripes
under the covers, something strange
is taking place inside me,
my tongue has turned to fur,
my head hums like something electric.

Yet by breakfast you would never know:
I fidget the toast around the plate,
it feels quite wrong
to eat honey on bee mornings.
Any minute I might take flight.

Feather Factory

We kiss by the side of the feather factory,
the stench of singed wings
fills our noses and mouths.

We are nest-bound – tongues entwined,
pockets full of Swan Vestas and Player's Number Six,
your nylon trousers spark to the rub.

Later the birds will haunt us:
their feathers will float around our heads,
pillow our eyes against the brightness of the day.

Family Values

Sun Daddy believed that the world was small

When the world knocked at his door
Sun Daddy put his head under the pillow
and shouted *go away.*

Every few weeks the world knocked
and Sun Daddy shouted,
and so it went on for years.

Sometimes when Sun Daddy was at work
Moon Mother invited the world in,
listened to its stories,

but made sure to shoo it out
before Sun Daddy's return.
One day Sun Daddy caught sight of the world

as it rolled away down the hill.

Sun Daddy's Moods

On good days Sun Daddy was the standard lamp,
he sat in the corner puffing away on his pipe.

The Star Children, their soft faces wreathed in smoke,
would creep nearer and nearer,

shuffling forwards on knees and bottoms,
daring each other to touch Sun Daddy's shoes.

But there was no telling
when Sun Daddy would change,

one wrong word could make his mood blacken,
and he would start to vibrate and hum,
like the electric carving knife.

The Song

Sun Daddy sang a song of women;
he sang it loud,
and with the insides of his pockets showing.

Sun Daddy's song was a song
of dark corners and cornfield fumbles.

The Star Children didn't understand the song,
but they felt its breath on their faces.

Sun Daddy's song had straw in its hair,
it rang the house on Christmas day
and left Moon Mother crying.

Sun Daddy liked to throw his pain around

He made Moon Mother
and the Star children suffer with him.

Moon Mother's suffering was too noisy,
so Sun Daddy locked her in the garage,

but when she had gone the younger
Star Children started fighting,

Sun Daddy clanged their heads
and sent them to their bedroom.

Star Girl was the only one left,
in her face Sun Daddy saw Moon Mother,

then he saw himself,
then he saw the size of his pain.

Sun Daddy invented the night

because, he said, *he couldn't trust the day,*
all its brightnesses.

He invented it full of shadowy corners,
he conjured nightmares and monsters.

The Star Children sweated under their nylon sheets,
they tried to light up the night with torches,

Star Girl, her radio pressed to her ear,
could almost convince herself night was day.

But Sun Daddy was wise to their mischief,
he dragged night back upstairs,

threw it into their bedroom and locked the door.

Broken

At Christmas Sun Daddy started smashing glass.

He started in his bedroom,
then swept tornado-like through the house:

windows, ornaments, glass lampshades,
the rented TV – nothing was safe.

When things quietened down,
they found him with his head on the kitchen table.

The room glittered around him.

Sun Daddy called a family meeting

the Star Children cowered around the table.

In family meetings Sun Daddy
was the only one allowed to speak.

The Star Children shivered
inside their cardigans.

The wind was high
but the storm had hardly begun.

When Moon Mother tried to leave

Sun Daddy held a gun to his head,
filled his cheeks with pills.

But you don't love me, whispered Moon Mother,
and I never did, blustered Sun Daddy.

Moon Mother went back into her kitchen and shut the door.
The Star Children peering through the bannisters,

saw Sun Daddy's triumphant dance,
saw him spit the tablets one by one along the hall.

Sun Daddy bought himself a pencil

it was a pencil of mythical proportions.

He drew Moon Mother and the Star children.

He drew himself a hole the size of the universe

and stepped into it.

Snow

Winter comes with the half-remembrance of rain
and the sudden opening out of the city,
a trail of footprints through unsullied whiteness,
where orange street light creates pools in icy gardens.

Tonight will freeze the city beneath a brittle crust,
wind the city down to slow:
as if the night raised a finger to hush us,
as if the sky whispered *no.*

Winter at Daniel's Hole

We camped there in summer evening heat;
tents pitched on tinder-dry grass
while we cooked beans and rice,
tore bread to wipe our wooden bowls,
to fill our bellies for sleep.

But winter is all box-shine,
glow-forth and tinsel-glint,
ice net-curtains the pond
and hardens the mud track
down to Daniel's Hole
where a boy once drowned,

sunk without a trace,
the blonde of his hair disappearing,
like birthing sped up and in reverse.
He's still there beneath the ice,
the sparkle of frost lighting up his face.

The Piano Lesson

When I asked Daddy if I could learn the piano, he said
NO because *MUSIC IS THE DEVIL'S WORK.* When
Daddy was away doing GOD'S WORK Mama took us
to visit the end-of-the-row neighbours. They are secret
friends because they are BAPTISTS. They have our house
back-to-front and a real live piano which sometimes I
am allowed to play. Steve taught me COCKLES AND
MUSSELS ALIVE ALIVE-O and in bed that night I sang
the song to Alice. I was just getting to the good bit about
the GHOST when Daddy banged in shouting *STOP THAT
NOISE, DON'T YOU KNOW THAT DUBLIN IS FULL OF
HEATHENS AND PAPISTS?* I didn't know what a papist
was, but I asked Daddy *is Molly Malone a Papist?* which
made Alice snort with laughter. Daddy didn't answer; he
just slammed out again muttering about Papists and the
devil. I hummed Cockles and Mussels under my breath
until I fell asleep, and that night I dreamt that I was Molly
Malone and my barrow looked a lot like a piano but with
limpets stuck all over it like the rocks on the beach at the
Sunday School outing.

Sisters (part ii)

vi.

This sister is the juice,
the blueberry burst of morning.
This sister has forsaken the bush
for the glamour of the bowl.

vii.

This sister is the undone,
the daughter of unravelled minds,
she is the curator in the quiet gallery of her past,
she is the one and one makes nine.

viii.

This sister is made of Lego,
she is primary-coloured with a petrol sheen,
she is studded for connection,
her instructions are numbered, easy to read.

ix.

This sister has neat borders,
she is carefully cultivated,
an exercise in quiet self-control.

x.

This sister is salt sea spray,
she rises up
throws herself against us,
smashes herself to bits.

xi.

This sister is the tang of onion on your fingers,
the persistent garlic on the Birds of Britain tea towel
that you wash and wash but cannot shift.

A Bird Inside

I wear a bird inside me:
a badge pinned to my heart,
drops of blood flower
where its pin pierces.

The bird inside me
opens its beak wide and sings:
I am full to the brim
with tweets and whistles.

I am made of spring
and I am raining,
wings feather my ears.

They are building
their nests inside my chest,
my head is full of grubs and worms.

Today I am blackbird,
tomorrow I will be all owl,
wearing a necklace of mouse skulls.

Quiet Man Norfolk

Like a baby dandled
on the knee of the sea
his shores cry *North, north.*

He feels polar breath
on runnelled cheeks
turns hunched back
on icy slop-stir.

Salt stings arthritic knees
while low-slung skies
look to flatten him,

mud and clay
clog his throat,
winter tides yank

but he clings tighter
his trousers a little shorter,
hems a little more ragged
than the year before.

Night Feed

My owl mother brings me mice nightly,
yanks me from the soft swoop of my dreams
to mustard-yellow streetlight.

I wake a-perch,
clench-clawed in the night-gloom,
my feathers bristling; rustling me from sleep.

Sun Sister:

a passing through,
a revisiting,
a pack carrier,
a ship's hold that exactly fits your past,
a hide,
a shelter,
the mouth empty of cadence,
how vowels fall soft like meadow grass
and speech smells of green, green, green.

Night Sickness

Her mother darns the window,
the moon leaks in
with its blue thumbprint.

The girl's legs splay on the bed.
She sleeps with a head full of horses:

sees her father at full gallop,
his massive hooves stomping over the countryside,
sees the sun toss its golden mane.

Her mother has nodded off in her chair –
she drops her silver needle with a clatter
but neither of them wakes.

The window unravels itself,
the night leaks slowly away.

Our Father as a Horse

Sister, last night I dreamt
our father jumped the fence
on that fenland holiday:
cleared it in one like a champion,
there was no holding him back.

He turned to face us
and the silver curl of his hair
framed his crinkled face.
A toss of his head sent his glasses skywards
as he galloped away across the field.

The Trap

I set the ALICE-TRAP at the top of the stairs hoping to trip her up and wait behind the top banister: squeezed between the wooden rails and the paraffin heater – which is off of course – we only use it in winter. Alice is a long time coming so I count spiders and then tick off all the boy's names I can think of on my fingers, and I have got to TWENTY-NINE, which is Frank, when I hear Alice come out of the kitchen, and Mama shouting *Go and wash your hands and you can help with dinner.* I AM SO EXCITED I imagine that I am the ferocious lion from Job about to POUNCE on my prey, and I fluff my hair up like a mane but it just flops down again. Then I try to get on all fours like a proper lion but the space is too small and the floor is all dusty, so I shuffle forwards on my bottom ready to SPRING OUT ON HER. I hear Alice's footsteps on the stairs, *pad-pad* – which is how I know it's her, because Daddy's walking is slower and heavier and Mama never comes upstairs. And as she gets nearer I stuff my fingers inside my mouth to stop myself squealing. THEN she steps on my trap and I pull the string and trip her up, and she is SHRIEKING and BAWLING and SPRAWLING on the landing with legs and arms OCTOPUSSING EVERYWHERE, and I jump out and surprise her with my lion paws and with VERY LOUD GROWLING. Then Mama comes out of the kitchen, her arms all dusty with flour and calls *What's going on up there? Do I need to fetch YOUR FATHER from the garden?* And Alice glares at me, and her look is like machine-gun-fire filling me full of holes and she says *No Mama I just TRIPPED that's all.* And to me she whispers *ME or GOD will get you later!* And Mama pushes her hair out of her eyes so that flour powders her cheek and goes right back into the steamy kitchen.

Definitions (i)

Sister:

an elongated O in the mouth of the morning

a throwing up of hands as if in horror

a reaching out

a tongue twister

a lie perpetuated

a click of double-jointed fingers

a wasp buzzing under a glass

arms clenched like a vice

an open hand

an isolation

From the Same Cloth

O daughter of the pine forest,
occupier of dark places,
you are prickly as a pine.
I spy on you in the mornings,
watch you dip your blackness
into the sun's frail light.
O dear one, ragged one,

you send your snaggle fingers down
into Breckland's thin soil,
snare rabbits in the net of your tresses.
When you are home
I watch you through the letterbox,
crunching bones and spitting out teeth.

Counterpoint

i.

two birds together
whose voices rise in song

ii.

one looks forward
the other looks back

iii.

on the one hand Robin
on the other Crow

iv.

how unbelonging
can feel like belonging

v.

to be outside yet inside
to be inside yet outside

vi.

how the same words sound
different in the mouth of another

Lent

We talked about spring babies, Whitsun weddings, Easter when it falls early and the time we found all the chocolate that Mama had GIVEN UP for Lent hidden in the bottom of the cleaning cupboard, and Mama cried and said *Please DON'T tell your Daddy*. But we liked to imagine his big hands resting on the faded skin of the BIBLE and his stern face and the *Mary you know you have done wrong!* Alice stole all that chocolate and we ate it up in the yard burying the silver foil underneath the compost heap where only JESUS can see it. Alice says JESUS can see everything – he can even see through walls. Sometimes I think about that when I'm in the bathroom, and Mamma is shouting *Come down stairs at once and go and get some potatoes* and Alice is whispering through the door *Hurry up in there, Mikey will be here soon and I need to get ready*. And then I remember how she KISSED Mikey in the car and I wonder why she isn't worried about JESUS seeing THAT and about the whole threat of MORTAL SIN. Mama says that autumn births are the worst because you have to go through the long hot summer, and Daddy puts his hand on the Holy Book and says *We won't talk of such things*. And then I remember the chocolate and how good it tasted and I am about to say something because I don't want to go to HELL, but Alice kicks me hard in the shin and I remember the sting of Daddy's hand. So when he looks at me with his caterpillar eyebrows raised THAT WAY I just lower my head and say nothing and know that presently we will eat dinner which will be ham and peas and potatoes, and I concentrate hard on my plate and imagine that I am JESUS and that I am eating up all the world's SIN.

Garden

Trying to make a garden
out of bird branches, nettles, dry grasses,
a wooden shed with slatted sides,
falling down and into itself.

Trying to alive a garden
out of weeds and light through leaves,
to grow a garden, to mound a garden
out of sycamore keys and thistle-prickle.

Trying to uncover a garden,
to mountain a garden out of goose grass, meadow-shine,
to weave a garden from stalk and stem,
from crows' wings and cloudlight.

Trying to Christmas a garden, to Easter a garden,
to flap a wing of a garden through
the stiff soldier arms of the trees,
to tangle a garden out of roots and worms,

to fox and owl a garden,
to slither a garden out of shadow,
to meow it, to cats-eye it out of night,
to hold a garden in a palm of light.

After identifying your body

We stagger into the cavernous dark
of a pub, weekday afternoon,
stale with beer and grease.
I watch the smoke curl up
from your mother's lips,
spiralling into light,
we drink I don't know what.

If you were here we'd be playing pool,
songs lined up on the jukebox,
drinks lined up on the bar,
the blue dust of cue chalk
powdering our hands.

But this day is slow motion,
and even though the sun glosses the grass
on Midsummer Common to a slick green foil
and the Cam shivers,
its dark body pinpricked with light,
I am somewhere else:

I am in the boat with the crew
rowing away from here as fast as I can.
And later I am sleeping
with a dog in a pub doorway,
my mouth sewn up with red thread,
your name tattooed across my face.

Water

i.

Water is an inside out,
a place and a nothingness,
it lives in the deep,
hides itself from everyone.

ii.

Water exposes itself,
lays everything bare.

iii.

I was of water
and I was empty.

iv.

Water was my teacher
but it taught me nothing.

v.

The day was snow
and later hail,
water was a clenched fist
hitting a bucket.

vi.

Water walked on stork legs
and sang in the valleys.

vii.

Water entered my dreams,
it watched me sleeping.

viii.

Water held a knife
to the throat of the village.

ix.

Water carried me
and broke me on the rocks.

x.

Water was a mirror,
but my breath could not fog it.

xi

Water was calypso
and the day was an orange.

xii

Water ate the city.

Yare Song

Marsh lover, mud flipper,
down amongst the groundlings,
moorhens, blue-lights,
sweet-shallow-mornings.

I am scaled and slithered:
strings of weed for hair,
dipping my shade-fingers
among bubbles and eddies,

spark-netted on the meanderings
of the mind's own river,
hearing the shadow-ghosts
of all those drowned girls: witches,

dipped down deep among
the slippery tendrils,
swan-necked lovelies
warbling in the reeds, singing.

Rain

Daddy said that the FLOODS were coming and we believed him – it rained for days and we didn't go out. Alice was grumpy because *the holidays were being wasted* but I didn't mind I LIKE staying indoors. I decided to get everything out of the cupboard in our room. First I found NOAH'S ARK and lined up all the animals, but some of them wouldn't stand up because they had broken legs. Next I played with Tiny Tears, but she couldn't cry anymore. Then I tried to draw an Ark on the Etch-a-sketch but I couldn't make the sides straight so I gave up and decided to find all my cuddly animals and get them ready for the REAL ARK. At dinner time on the fifth day of rain Daddy said that *ALL THE SINNERS IN THE WORLD WOULD DROWN AND GOOD RIDDANCE,* and I held Easter Bunny tight between my knees so he knew I would save him, and so that Daddy would not make me take him back upstairs because *WE ARE NOT ALLOWED TOYS AT THE TABLE.* That night I had a nightmare about water coming in the window and I woke up screaming. Mama said to Daddy *NOW look what you've done!* And she gave me a glass of milk and a biscuit even though we aren't allowed to eat in bed. I saved the biscuit under my pillow because there won't be much food on the Ark. When they had gone I couldn't get back to sleep – I was too busy remembering all the BAD THINGS that I had done like writing POO in the back of a school book, and I decided that I would have to build MY OWN ARK in case Daddy couldn't save me. I must have fallen asleep praying because the next minute the SUN was shining and Alice was bouncing on my bed saying *Get up Lazy Bones the rain's gone, and Mama says if we clear up we can go to the shops!* And I knew that my prayers HAD been answered, and that I should try hard not to sin anymore. But I DID want some sweets, and as Mama says I AM ONLY A CHILD, so I kicked the mess under Alice's bed, and wondered whether Daddy would buy me a new Tiny Tears if I accidently broke her arm off, because if I'm not going to die yet I WOULD like a doll who can REALLY CRY!

The Drunkenness of Noah

The after-school surprise
is seeing you sprawled
on the hall floor in broad daylight,

the top half of your body
in the downstairs lav,
Mum tugging uselessly on your feet,

you like one of those giant seals
we saw on the beach at Easter,
floundering on the sand.

I imagine the blue and black
tiled floor as the ocean,
that when the tide rises

you will twist and dive,
your cumbersome body
light and fast as a fish.

Definitions (ii)

Sisterhood:

a leaning inwards

a holding up

a carrying

a full cup

an overgrown path   that sometimes leads to a clearing

a single sustained note

an unfulfilled promise

an open door

Thetford Forest

Frozen mud-pelt of early morning,
the air bristles with frost-shine.

Our winter breath hangs
in the air before us.

We walk into deep grey
where the trees crowd in,

their pine needle smell
overwhelming.

There is faraway bird-call,
the startled flap of a fresh waked pigeon.

A deer eye appears,
and vanishes back into shadow.

We emerge into the stark-limbed skeleton
of the deciduous forest.

The sky opens out – a gap of relief
after the inky conifers.

We gulp lung after lung of early winter,
see every third tree marked with a cross:

a yellow smear
where the saw will bite,

flaking jackets of bark barely
covering pale bodies.

Something About the Light

reminded her of something just out of reach.

Something urban: the repetition of flat roofs,
the way street lights dimmed at ten to one
throwing her room into sudden darkness,
the possibility of a kiss, gravel rain on a wooden roof
or the relentless thup, thup of ping pong balls
above the summer disco of Radio One.

Something alive: fireworks
lighting up the estate like the Blitz,
the Thermos factory siren calling out the men.
And always the quiet thrum of traffic,
far away and London bound,
and the crack, crack, crack
of the rifle range beyond the wall of pines.

The Callers

The day the Jehovah's Witnesses knocked at the door was the same day that Alice fell in the river. Daddy made us all say extra prayers after dinner to give thanks. I opened my eyes during prayers and Alice pinched me, and although I was glad she was saved, part of me really wanted her top bunk, which I know is COVETOUSNESS and is a SIN. After tea Alice and I went to play ball-against-the-wall in the garden, but a daddy longlegs got caught in my hair. Alice said I wasn't allowed to kill it because *IT IS ONE OF GOD'S CREATURES* and it was getting dark anyway so I decided to go indoors. In the hall the cat was trapping moths with her prickly paws and chewing them up with a noise like bacon frying. I was going to chase her outside but just then someone knocked loudly at the front door – FLAP, FLAP REALLY HARD ON THE LETTERBOX. Mama shouted *Ruthie can you answer that?* So I pulled the door open and found two really tall men standing there. They were wearing extra smart suits – like for a wedding, and very big smiles. One of them crouched down to talk to me and his hair was shiny like the shine you get on cheese on toast, and he said *I'm very pleased to meet you missy, my name's Andy, are your mummy or daddy at home?* And I said *My name's NOT Missy and you don't need to crouch down I'M NOT A TODDLER*, and I went to fetch Daddy who was annoyed to be disturbed because he was watching the news, which is A SERIOUS BUSINESS. When Daddy came to the door the crouchy man stood up and shook his hand. He asked Daddy if he had ever heard *THE WORD OF JEHOVAH*, and he called Daddy *Sir* even though he isn't a teacher. I thought that Daddy would shut the door on him, but instead he opened it even wider and smiled a huge smile that was REALLY SCARY, and rubbed his hands together like right before he carves the turkey, and he said *I DON'T BELIEVE I HAVE – STEP RIGHT INSIDE GENTLEMEN.*

Gin Fox

The bar man sniffs me quietly
sensing something awry.
The glass is always half-full for me,
he later tells me as he unhooks
my bra in a dirty alley.
I smile into the frosty darkness.
I've been here before and know
I must keep my sharp teeth
under wraps. But I'm easily bored,
and the gin is wearing off.
I press my paws into his pockets,
rub my muzzle against his face,
try to steal a little warmth.
He is panting now, and he is struggling
with my buttons, biting at my neck,
yanking my skirt a little too high
until it releases
the full glory of my tail.

Moldewarpe

Black-slinked in the night
he ruffles, with shovel hands
and a nose bent upwards
to propel him.
Slovenly yet precise
he mountains dirt in the meadow,
holes through soil-slub,
rummages with his flat pinks –
swivels rooms and tunnels.

Slick black engineer
in dug-outs and trenches;
pin-eyed earth-thrower
with a stomach full of cut-worms,
wire-worms, leather-jackets,
manning his own vertical empire
of things that dance and crawl.
Soft-pelted soldier,
fight-to-the-death pest.

Sparrow Sister

You are nothing to me hisses Sister,
lifting her beak from the plate,
her bead eyes glinting.
I feel a tear welling but blink it back,

step through the French doors
and into her pocket-sized garden,
kneel in the scuffed-up grass
and start digging for worms.

Oak

It was as if we had ensnared ourselves:
the way your little boy hands
pushed the acorn into the soft loam
and your face looked up to mine
with the unspoken question.
And later a green finger
pushed itself out of the earth
and you measured it year by year,
until gradually the slender stem
became entwined with the fence
and the only way to separate them
would be to take a knife and cut them apart.

My owl sister mistakes me for a mouse

I let myself go slack in her claws.
Her wings soft the air,

hang us in deep blue brushed with stars,
the village spreads below like a painting.

I try to speak her name
but all I manage is a squeak.

She dives low over the farm,
drops me through a chimney hole

in amongst her needle-beaked children.
She doesn't pause or look back.

My owl sister pays me a visit

She moves restlessly around the room
examining every object, flexes her wings,

lingers by the double-glazed window,
shields her eyes as if the day is too bright.

I know she hates hospitals,
and I have interrupted her schedule,

she has chicks to feed,
important things to do.

She plucks a vole from her breast pocket,
and drops it onto my blanket,

turns on her claw.
Her hoot echoes along the ward.

Clearing Out Mum

It's like unreeling
yards and yards of tangled wire,
or finding mice in an attic
you never even knew you had.
It's the wash-off, run-through,
bleed-right hours of sorting.

It's like squirreling backwards,
or finding yourself back in the town
that you spent years getting out of.
It's a thousand keys without a lock,
(or a thousand locks without a key).

It's the unravelled jumper syndrome
of clutter-mouth, skip-face, charity-bone.
It's those sweets in a bowl that your Nana saved.
It's the pencilled words in the book
that you gave your mother and she defaced.

It's like a shoe-shine crystal avalanche,
it's hair on a brush and teeth in a bag,
it's a dirty bathroom and unwashed plates,
an amalgamation of days and nights and nights and days.

After cleaning out your house

I wanted to rush home and throw everything away,
cram it all into bin bags.
I wanted to mix letters
with plates and underwear,
sweep them, like a bonfire waiting for a match,
into the middle of the floor.
I wanted to open up the house wide,
invite the wind and the trees inside.
I wanted to throw away the windows,
the doors, the front path, the weeds,
the cars, the people walking along the street,
turn the kitchen cupboards inside out,
uncook all those breakfasts and dinners,
turn on the taps until the water ran dry.

Visiting Time

When Mama was in hospital we went to visit her and took lilies tied with ribbon and chocolates in a shiny gold box. Mama couldn't eat the chocolates so Alice and I ate them. The old lady in the next bed gave us her chocolates too because she didn't have any teeth, and they were the ones in the Black Magic Box like on the advert. Daddy made us give those ones back because Black Magic is *THE DEVIL'S WORK*. In the hospital all the nurses called Mama Anna, which made her smile. On the way home Daddy had to stop the car so I could be sick and Alice held my hair. Daddy said that being sick was my punishment for GLUTTONY. When we got home I was feeling AS BRAVE AS A BEAR and while we were hanging up our coats I said to Daddy: *Why do you call Mama Mary when her name is Anna?* Alice made a sign of a knife across the throat, and Daddy banged his fist on the banister and shouted: *DOES YOUR MOUTH NEED THE SOAP?* Alice ran into the toilet and locked the door, which is very stupid because you have to come out sometime. I sat on the stairs and waited for the soap, but instead Daddy brought cloths and polish and told me to clean all the shoes in the house so that my IDLE HANDS would keep out of trouble, and then he went into his office with the Bible and shut the door. Alice came out of the toilet and sat on the next step down. I put on the polish with a green flowery cloth made from my old school dress and Alice took the hedgehog brush and we made all those shoes REALLY SHINE.

Operation

The fear is the clock on the wall,
it's the cold,
the pulling fast and through,
it's a bed with needles,
it is lying still and pretending not to notice.

The dream is to take up your bed and walk,
it is a long thin waiting
followed by fat days of celebration.

The fear is everything and nothing,
it is living the nightmare
you had the day before yesterday,
it is made of tubes and ties up at the back,
it wears a dressing gown and slippers.

Maternity Ward

Like a flower when the first frost comes –
she is shut up tight, pressed into herself,

her ears are full of ringing phones
and raised voices: a curtain of sound,

while her own mouth emits
a series of beeps and whistles.

In between meals she watches the baby,
trying hard to understand it,

its arms and legs move jerkily
and its mouth howls open.

She can't distinguish friendly faces, can't be sure
if real life exists within the room or outside it,

the bed has wheels –
it drives her away while she is sleeping.

The Miracle

Daddy says the new baby is a MIRACLE, but Alice says she came because Mama and Daddy had SEX. We learned about S-E-X at school and there is no way Mama and Daddy would do THAT. For a start for S-E-X you have to be naked and I am sure that Daddy sleeps with all his clothes on – including his shoes – although I can't prove it because we are not allowed in Mama and Daddy's room. Mama keeps BABY very close as if she might lose her, and she has new less friendly eyes for me and Alice. She would sleep in Baby's room if Daddy would allow it, but of course he won't. *Mary* he says, *the place of a wife is at her husband's side.* I wouldn't mind the baby sleeping in MAMA'S room – because then we wouldn't have to hear it crying. Alice says that I used to cry all the time too and that I should be more sympathetic, and she asks why I am still calling her Baby and not Hannah. Baby is less than a month old and she already has her own room and I have been waiting SEVEN YEARS! And anyway everyone knows that babies aren't real until they have been baptised – until then their soul belongs to THE DEVIL. Daddy says she will be baptised very soon and I cross my fingers behind my back and hope that he will change his mind and send that Miracle right back where it came from.

Breakdown

i.

One mistake
was all it took
for things to start to unravel,
and there is one place left
in the car park if only we can find it;
we drive round and round
for minutes that feel like hours.

ii.

Two days of bliss
before the rows kick in,
followed by the silent treatment,
that jolt on waking,
the stomach flipping and bucking.

iii.

Go straight to the nub, the way
weeds have taken over the garden so quickly
as if there were never any neat borders,
and keep all those holiday snaps
on your old laptop, no need to print them out.

iv.

And we have to discuss
how you said her name
that time on holiday in Lewes,
the tulip-red of your face,
the way your eyes slid
downwards and sideways –
things get uncomfortable.

v.

I try to map my way out of this mess
through the cups and cutlery,
tables placed too close together,

the unsettling chirps of laughter,
you impassively staring
at the foam-rimmed cup,

and here we are emptied of each other,
so empty there's nothing
but the chink of crockery.

I have forgotten my password to you

I have made too many login attempts and you have locked me out.
When I request a password reset you say my username is invalid.
Someone else has tried to hack their way in or access my login.
My account has been locked because of too many failed attempts.
Some one or thing is trying to hack the admin.
You tell me to try again in 24 hours. This is a huge problem.
It would be helpful to know the location of the lockout threshold
    settings.
A locked account cannot be used until it is reset by an
    administrator.
There is no longer a default unlocking option.

no one speaks of you

unless they don't know not to speak of you
and those who know not to speak of you
and have to speak of you
speak of you in hushed voices
as if you're a baby asleep in their arms
and those who don't know not to speak of you
speak of you loudly almost shouting
as if your name is a triumph a hallelujah
and when I tell them that I don't know how you are
that I haven't seen you for months
they reel back as if they are the ones hurt
and I know that the next time we meet
they won't speak of you and if they do
it will be quietly and seriously

This is how to fall

Balance yourself on the edge,
close your eyes to the river, the mud,
the to and fro of cars on the road below.

Draw a soft breath of resolve,
puff your chest out like a bird,
stretch out your arms and take flight.

Drop into something mid-way
between a tumble and glide,
feel the air tug at your skin and clothes,

the cold rush of wind.
Hear the world's almost silence,
the secret whistle that only the falling hear.

Bee Dress

Give me a dress made of honeybees
that I will wear in humming praise of summer,
that shimmies its blacks and yellows
across my body in waves,
each curve of bee a buzzing bead
that catches the sun's rays as I move.

Let the whole street see my waggle dance
as my bee dress swarms and sings –
lifts me clear above the pavement,
leaving behind me a fine yellow dust,
a faint whiff of honey.

Tickets to the Circus

Magician

Sister is a magician:
her sleeves are stuffed
with brightly coloured scarves,
her pockets are full of doves,
tiny balls make hamster pouches of her cheeks.

I watch her from my bedroom window
disappearing my pet rabbit,
her white wand-tip flickering in the dusk.

Bearded Woman

Sister makes me the dancing horse,
she cracks the whip in time to the music,
stands one-legged on my back.

I pick my hooves up delicately
avoiding the clothes and books
on the bedroom floor.

Game over, she hugs me tightly,
squashes the air right out of my chest,
scratches my face with the Brillo pad of her beard.

Knife Thrower

Today it's the knives
and I know I have to keep very still,
she paces the room,
face contorted with concentration.
I close my eyes and wait to feel
the blade's soft wind kiss my skin.

Fire Breather

I wake in the night to light
flickering across my eyelids,
see Sister silhouetted
against the open window.
She opens her mouth,
breathes out a long tongue of flame.

Siamese Twins

Sister and I wake as Siamese twins:
getting dressed is a two-headed, four-legged dance,
there is a fight to use the toilet first.

In the kitchen we push two chairs together,
share the same bowl with two spoons.

Getting through doorways is the biggest problem,
we perfect the crab-walk, skitter sideways,
carefully avoid each other's claws.

Contortionist

I never tire of seeing her bottom
above her head, her face framed
by the right angles of her knees.

Dancing Bear

Sister slips the collar and chain around my neck
and I lumber up out of bed yowling.

Sister is a kind mistress: she allows me breakfast
and doesn't tug too hard on the chain.

Trapeze

Sister glides down from the ceiling
and hangs upside down above my bed.

*Grab my hands and I'll fly you
to the sun,* she says.

Sword Swallower

Sunday lunch and Mum sends me to see
why Sister is taking so long in the kitchen.

I push the door open and enter,
my furry slippers quiet as cat paws,

watch the bread knife disappear
up to its handle down Sister's throat.

Acknowledgements

Many thanks to the editors of the following journals, anthologies and websites where some of these poems have appeared (sometimes in earlier incarnations): *And Other Poems; Clear Poetry; Ink, Sweat and Tears; Literary Norfolk; Magma; Obsessed With Pipework; Other Poetry; Poems in the Waiting Room; Poetry Salzburg Review; Poetry Spotlight; Poetry Unbound; Ten Poets: UEA Poetry 2010; The Poetry Shed; The Fenland Reed; The Inflectionist Review; The Inflectionist Review Anthology; The Rialto; Twelve Slanted Poems for Christmas; Wherryman's Web* and *Your One Phone Call.* 'Lent' won the Poetry Society's 2011 Stanza Competition.

C.D. Williams quote from *The Poet, The Lion, Talking Pictures, El Farolito, A Wedding in St. Roch, The Big Box Store, The Warp in the Mirror, Spring, Midnights, Fire & All* (published by Copper Canyon Press, 2016).

I would like to thank: the poetry tutors who set me on the path – George Szirtes, Helen Ivory, Andrea Holland, Martin Figura and Lavinia Greenlaw; members (past and present) of the workshopping groups who helped me knock some of these poems into shape especially: Laura Elliott, Angus Sinclair, Mike Saunders, Christopher Tracey, Jo Surzyn, Katherine Venn, Heidi Williamson, Helen Ivory, Martin Figura, Anne Osbourn, Ramona Herdman, Lynn Woollacott, Richard Lambert, Meryl Pugh, Stuart Charlesworth, Peter Wallis, Laura Scott, Theo Best, Sally Festing and Caroline Gilfilian. Special thanks to: Arts Council England for a Grant for the Arts, UEA for a Malcolm Bradbury Continuation Grant; The Arvon Foundation for an Arvon 42 grant; to Pascale Petit for her brilliant mentorship and George Szirtes for his continued encouragement and support. I would also like to thank everyone who has believed in my work – especially Jane Commane at Nine Arches Press.